IMAGES
of America

MARINE CORPS
RECRUIT DEPOT
SAN DIEGO

ON THE COVER: C COMPANY, 4TH PLATOON, 1923. These recruits were among the first to be trained in San Diego. This particular platoon was selected as the Honor Platoon for their superior achievement. Pictured here just days away from graduation, these men came with the first wave of 250 recruits aboard the transport ship USS *Sirius* on August 12, 1923, under the command of Lt. G.L. Gloeckner.

IMAGES
of America

MARINE CORPS RECRUIT DEPOT SAN DIEGO

Matthew J. Morrison and Paul J. Richardson

ARCADIA
PUBLISHING

Published by Arcadia Publishing
Charleston, South Carolina

Printed in the United States of America

Library of Congress Control Number: 2011928023

For all general information, please contact Arcadia Publishing:
Telephone 843-853-2070
Fax 843-853-0044
E-mail sales@arcadiapublishing.com
For customer service and orders:
Toll-Free 1-888-313-2665

Visit us on the Internet at www.arcadiapublishing.com

To all the Marines made in San Diego
and those who are yet to be.
Semper Fidelis.

CONTENTS

ACKNOWLEDGMENTS

Marine Corps Recruit Depot (MCRD) San Diego is where we became Marines. Few pieces of ground hold such an important place in the heart of a Marine as his "second birthplace." The memories are strong, and they are certainly always a mix of pleasure and pain. In this case, it was with great pleasure that we explored the depot once again and are able to share its colorful history.

The greatest thanks goes to the staff at the Command Museum at MCRD San Diego. In particular, we want to thank Ellen Guillemette for taking the time to answer our questions, searching through old photographs with and for us, and generally putting up with us. Another special thank-you goes to museum director Barbara McCurtis. We are grateful to have such a wonderful resource in the museum. Faye Jonason and her staff at the Camp Pendleton History Division were also significant contributors to our success, providing us with additional photographs and historical insight.

Our long-distance contributors also deserve recognition; the US Naval Observatory Library and the Naval History and Heritage Command. Bob Holmes of Osage Beach, Missouri, was also kind enough to provide a personal photograph.

Dr. Mike Moodian, a mutual professor of ours at Chapman University, served as the initial inspiration for writing this book. His previous work in the same series, *Rancho Santa Margarita*, is what gave us the idea in the first place. Thanks to an incredibly talented brother-in-law, Michael Vaughn of Mackel Vaughn Photography (www.mackelvaughnphotography.com) in Orange County, California, who went to MCRD with us to recreate the cover photograph and take some other great shots.

Everyone at Arcadia Publishing deserves our sincere gratitude, but in particular we would like to thank Debbie Seracini, Amy Perryman, and Jerry Roberts. Jerry took us through the proposal and acquisitions phase quite quickly and painlessly. Debbie and Amy, our project editors, were fantastic. It can be a task trying to rein in a couple of Marine sergeants, but they did so with a fine balance of graciousness and encouragement. Gracious also describes our two staff noncommissioned officers at Camp Pendleton who were good enough to allow us time off to conduct research in San Diego and sometimes do "a little" bit of writing during working hours. Thank you, Gunnery Sergeant Tracy Gipson and Staff Sergeant John Osborn.

Finally, we must thank our families. Our wives, Lindsey Morrison and Aracely Richardson, have been a tremendous blessing and support throughout this project.

Photographs from the Command Museum are credited as MCRD.

Photographs from the Naval History and Heritage Command are credited as USNHHC.

INTRODUCTION

The Marine presence in San Diego was first established in 1846 when, during the Mexican-American War, the USS *Cyane* sent aground a detachment of Marines and sailors to seize the town. The American flag was first raised in Southern California over Old Town Plaza during that operation. At the conclusion of the war in 1848, the Marines departed, not to return in force for over 60 years.

More unrest in Mexico brought the Marines back to San Diego. Following a corrupt election in 1910, Mexico was in the throes of a revolution that eventually prompted President Taft to dispatch a military show of force along the border, under the auspices of a training exercise. On March 20, 1911, the Marines landed in San Diego on North Island and established Camp Thomas, named in honor of Adm. Chauncey Thomas, who was the Pacific Fleet commander at that time. Things in Mexico calmed down within a few months, and the regiment encamped on North Island eventually disbanded.

Peace in Mexico was not to last, as another shift in Mexico's leadership created a strained relationship with the United States once again. Things worsened in 1914, after American naval personnel, having been mistreated by Mexican officials at Tampico, were refused an apology for said treatment. When the United States learned that a shipment of military supplies was bound for Veracruz, President Wilson ordered the delivery prevented and Veracruz was soon seized. At the same time that Marines were landing at Veracruz, the 4th Marine Regiment was assembled and aboard ships heading for the Gulf of California as an additional show of force. The 4th Marines never went ashore and were instead ordered home late that June. It was expected that the regiment would once again be disbanded, but San Diego was under consideration as an advance base station for the Marine Corps, so the regiment took up camp on North Island once again. This camp was again named in honor of the current Pacific Fleet commander, Adm. Thomas Howard.

Initially, the consideration of San Diego for an advance base was spurred on by an April 1914 visit to the area by then assistant secretary of the navy Franklin Delano Roosevelt. The idea to station Marines permanently in San Diego was not without opposition, though. The commandant of the Marine Corps at the time, Maj. Gen. George Barnett, was in favor of placing a base nearer the center of the recruiting district (in San Francisco) like Mare Island, stating that the only thing San Diego had going for it was the good weather and that the costs associated with ground-up construction would be too prohibitive. There were two men, though, who felt differently.

Local US congressman William Kettner and Col. Joseph Pendleton were the strongest advocates for the San Diego Marine base. Elected in 1912, Kettner immediately began the work that would eventually earn him the title "Father of San Diego's Navy." Kettner had secured funding for multiple projects, including deepening the harbor for larger vessels and construction of several naval facilities. Colonel Pendleton, in the meantime, had been making quite an effort to establish meaningful relationships between the Marines and the people of San Diego. He would often make speeches around town and hosted an open house aboard Camp Howard two or more times a week, in which he would put on colorful pageants and Marine parades. The regiment at Camp Howard was soon split in two and assigned to exposition duty in San Diego and San Francisco. The displays and demonstrations put on by the Marines further endeared them to the people of San Diego.

In the spring of 1915, just months after assignment to exposition duty, Colonel Pendleton approached Kettner about the idea of a permanent Marine base. Although skeptical at first, Kettner was eventually won over and even proposed a parcel of land for the base known as Dutch Flats. This low tidal land was more than likely Kettner's choice, because it was in perfect view of his house atop Horton's Hill. General Barnett eventually came around after a personal site survey in the summer of 1915. He concluded that the Dutch Flats area and some more adjacent land would be well suited to an advance base and that weather, again, was very good for year-round work and training.

Later that year, San Diego deeded an additional 500 acres of tidal land to the Navy for base construction. After the land was paid for in June 1917, it would be another two years before construction of the base actually began. World War I was in full swing. While dredging and filling operations were in progress, it was not until March 15, 1919, that the official ground breaking took place. The design of the base was in the hands of skilled architect and illustrator Bertram Goodhue. The Spanish Colonial Revival style was a nod to the history of the region and garnered a great deal of praise from everyone who saw it. General Pendleton declared that the San Diego base would be "the most beautiful and picturesque military post in the United States." On December 1, 1921, General Pendleton raised the flag over his new and most beautiful base for the first time.

Construction continued on the base, and on August 2, 1923, the West Coast Recruit Training Station relocated from Mare Island to San Diego. This marked the beginning of the San Diego base legacy of recruit training. Also coming to San Diego with recruit training were Sea School and its subordinate, Field Music School. The next several years brought a great deal of change to the base, although not as much in the way of facilities, but rather by tenants and commands. In spring of 1924, the base was redesignated Marine Corps Base, Naval Operating Base, San Diego, much to the chagrin of General Pendleton, who had previously fought to keep the new base independent of the Navy. In 1927, the base was the staging ground for expeditionary service in China, and the name of the Recruit Training Station was changed to Recruit Depot San Diego. The following years saw the basing of engineer, artillery, headquarters, and casual units as well as the newly established Fleet Marine Force (FMF).

The many conflicts our nation has since been a part of played pivotal roles in the shaping and use of the San Diego base. Construction boomed during World War II and saw the establishment and closing of multiple schools and the forming of many outlying, subordinate training camps and bases such as La Jolla, Dunlap, Gillespie, Matthews, and Elliot. The end of World War II brought a large reduction in force and, with it, the scaled down role of the San Diego base. In 1948, the base was officially given its current name, Marine Corps Recruit Depot San Diego, and recruit training became the primary focus, continuing to this very day.

One

FOUNDATION OF A LEGACY
1911–1922

The fight to bring the Marines to San Diego for good was not an easy one. With the steadfast devotion of Col. Joseph Pendleton, the hearts of minds of the local population were quickly won over, but it would take an ally in Washington, DC, to open the wallet and make the dream a reality. That friend in Washington was a sophomore congressman by the name of William Kettner, who would go on to be known as the "Father of San Diego's Navy."

CENTER ARCH. One of the many arches along the 1,000-foot-long arcade, this arch is the centerpiece that epitomizes the Spanish Colonial Revival–style architecture of Bertram Goodhue. Goodhue also was a key architect in the Panama-California Exposition at Balboa Park. The Eagle, Globe, and Anchor, the official emblem of the Marine Corps, was cast with a giant five-foot eagle. (MCRD.)

ADMIRAL THOMAS. Rear Adm. Chauncey Thomas Jr. (first row, center) graduated from the US Naval Academy in 1871 and commissioned as an ensign. He assumed command of the Pacific Fleet in 1910. The following year, when Marines of the 4th Provisional Regiment landed in San Diego, they named their site Camp Thomas after him. This was the first of many encampments that led to the creation of MCRD San Diego. (USNHHC.)

FIRST CAMP. Camp Thomas was established on March 20, 1911, by the 4th Provisional Marine Regiment on North Island, San Diego. This was the first time the Marines had been in Southern California since the Mexican American War in 1848. The Marines occupied this camp for nearly three months, all the while earning the admiration of the Pacific Fleet commander and the *San Diego Union* newspaper, which declared that "it would be impossible to find a camp which compares to that of the Marines." In 1911, tensions in Mexico, which had brought the Marines to the area originally, subsided quickly and the regiment was dissolved. Camp Thomas was abandoned in July of that year. (Both, MCRD.)

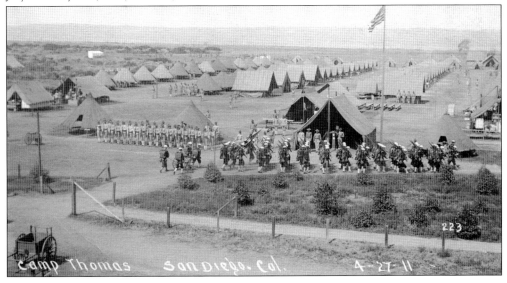

FIRST COMMANDER. Brig. Gen. Charles A. Doyen was commander of Marine Barracks Puget Sound and 4th Provisional Marine Brigade. As a colonel, Doyen commanded the first Marine Corps unit to establish formal camp in the San Diego area. The 4th Marines set up Camp Thomas on North Island under Doyen, who went on to become the first Marine officer to command a US Army unit (World War I). (MCRD.)

ADMIRAL HOWARD. In 1914, Rear Admiral Howard replaced Admiral Thomas as the commander of the US Pacific Fleet. With such influence over the West Coast naval operations, the Marines named their next camp on North Island after him. Camp Howard had only been established for less than a year when the Marines moved to Balboa Park. (USNHHC.)

GENERAL BARNETT. Maj. Gen. George Barnett was commandant of the Marine Corps from 1916 to 1920. General Barnett was among those initially against establishing a base in San Diego. Barnett testified before the House Naval Affairs Committee, indicating that he felt that the current facility at Mare Island, near San Francisco, was more appropriate due to its proximity to the center of the recruiting district. He reasoned that the amount of money required to send new recruits from San Francisco to San Diego and back again when they were needed would not be financially sound. After being continually pressured to pay a visit to San Diego in the summer of 1915, Barnett finally conceded that San Diego was "well suited" for an advance base because of the good weather and San Diego being the southernmost harbor on the Pacific Coast. (MCRD.)

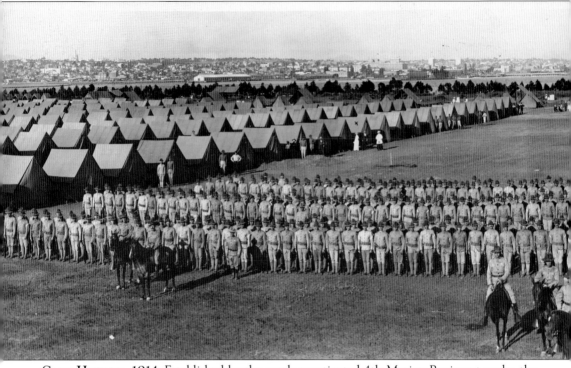

CAMP HOWARD, 1914. Established by the newly reactivated 4th Marine Regiment under the command of Col. Joseph Pendleton, Camp Howard was named for the commander of the Pacific Fleet at that time and was erected on the same site as Camp Thomas in 1911. The 4th Marines had previously spent two months anchored at various Mexican ports anticipating clashes with

COLONEL PENDLETON, 1912. Promoted to colonel in May 1911, Pendleton was given command of the 4th Marine Regiment in 1914. Pendleton and his men boarded the USS *South Dakota* and USS *Jupiter* and steamed for San Diego. They arrived in July 1914 and landed on North Island, naming their bivouac site Camp Howard. (MCRD.)

Mexican forces, which never came. The Marines instead steamed north and waited in San Diego, fully expecting to be disbanded. Because San Diego was in consideration as a potential site for a Marine Corps advance base, the regiment was maintained and assigned to exposition duty in San Francisco and San Diego. (MCRD.)

MARINE BARRACKS, PUGET SOUND. Until the late 19th century, there was no formal structure for training Marine recruits. General Biddle formed the first official training bases in 1911, with two on the West Coast. The first was at Puget Sound in Washington State. Puget Sound was short-lived, however, as it was combined with the more centrally located training facility at Mare Island near San Francisco. (USNHHC.)

DUTCH FLATS, 1915. Dutch Flats, pictured above on January 24, 1919, was the spot favored by Congressman William Kettner for the location of the San Diego base. Although this area was nothing more than a low-lying marsh covered by water at high tide, extensive dredging and filling would soon transform it into a suitable foundation for the largest construction project the Marine Corps had authorized. Below is the same area several months later as dredging and filling operations began to transform the marsh into workable land. Barnett Avenue can be seen in the background running below the power lines. (Both, MCRD.)

CONGRESSMAN KETTNER. William Kettner was a US congressman from San Diego from 1913 to 1921. He is considered the "Father of San Diego's Navy" for all the work he did legislating on behalf of the Navy and Marine Corps. During his first two-year term in office, Kettner was able to secure over $650,000 for naval projects, such as deepening San Diego's harbor, a coal wharf and fuel station on Point Loma, and a Navy radio station. The congressman's big push for the Marine base came when the bill that he authored for the funding of the Marine base was passed and the provisions were incorporated into the 1916 Naval Appropriations Act. Kettner referred to MCRD as "my baby, and I want it to stand as a monument of my works in Congress for the City of San Diego." (Library of Congress.)

MARE ISLAND. Recruit training slowly made its way southward after the consolidation of the Puget Sound facility. All new Marine recruits from the West Coast were trained at Mare Island in the San Francisco Bay Area until 1923, when the depot was moved to San Diego. Above is a barracks building with bayonet course in the foreground. Several of these buildings are still standing today, although the whole naval base was closed in 1995. San Pablo Bay can be seen in the distance. Left, a young recruit poses with his M1903 Springfield rifle. The M1903 was such a robust and accurate bolt-action rifle that it stayed in service in various forms through the Vietnam War. (Both, MCRD.)

CABRILLO BRIDGE, 1915. Marines of the 4th Regiment march over the Cabrillo Bridge from Balboa Park, site of the Panama-California Exposition. The regiment, future residents of MCRD, were only on exposition duty for a few months before being called to service in Mexico again. The bridge upon which they are marching had just recently been completed for the exposition. (MCRD.)

POINT LOMA, 1915. In a mutually beneficial exercise, Colonel Pendleton provided Marines as security guards for the popular Point Loma Road Race. The race organizers knew the Marines would maintain good order, and Colonel Pendleton knew he could use the event to highlight Marines in San Diego to help gain favor to establish a permanent base there. (MCRD.)

PANAMA-CALIFORNIA EXPOSITION. When the Panama Canal was completed in 1914, San Diego held an exposition in Balboa Park to commemorate the event. Marines from the 4th Regiment were assigned to exposition duty and remained there until MCRD opened in 1921. They were ordered to maintain model camps to display Marine discipline and uniformity. It also served to help Colonel Pendleton persuade the people of San Diego to keep a Marine base there permanently. Above, Marines stand at attention in their battle uniforms. Below, Marines wearing their dress blue uniforms stand in formation as the impressed San Diego population watches in awe. (Both, MCRD.)

MODEL MARINE CORPS CAMP, 1915. The 2nd Battalion of the 4th Marine Regiment from Camp Howard was assigned to exposition duty for the Panama-California Exposition, which opened in Balboa Park on January 1, 1915. The Marines at Balboa maintained a working camp in a pristine condition to showcase the efficiency of the Corps in addition to normal daily drills and inspections. The regimental band would also put on concerts at the Spreckels pavilion. Colonel Pendleton moved the Regimental headquarters to Balboa and officially established Marine Barracks, Balboa Park. The Marines would remain here for several years after the exposition ended, until Marine Corps Base San Diego was officially opened in 1921. (Both, MCRD.)

PARADE GROUND AND ARCADE, 1920. Above, the east end of the arcade, to include barracks A-1 (center) and C-1 (right), and parade ground, was the first structure of the base to be built. This photograph shows the completely ungraded dirt surface that will eventually be the parade grounds and the raw brick structure of the barracks and arcade before application of stucco. The July 1920 photograph below looks west from C-1 at barracks A-2 through A-6. Architect Bertram Goodhue's original plan called for just fewer than 50 buildings on 50 acres, with the rest of the land for a parade ground, athletic field, and possible aviation space. At the time of approval, the estimated cost to complete the project was $5 million. (Both, MCRD.)

INITIAL CONSTRUCTION. On November 29, 1919, Dutch Flats was beginning to take shape with the erection of temporary storage buildings and a construction office. These building were later removed as construction was completed. In the background is what is now known as the Mission Hills area of San Diego, just south of Old Town. (MCRD.)

LOOKING EAST. What would become the base parade ground is being filled and graded with sandy soil from the nearby dredged harbor in this photograph taken July 1, 1921. Because of the time it took for the high salt content in the soil used to fill Dutch Flats to leech out, it would be several years before proper landscaping could be done. (MCRD.)

CONSTRUCTION MATERIAL IN COURTYARD, 1920. A system of ramps and walkways was used to transport materials, including the cinder blocks on the right, to the upper floor of the building that today houses the MCRD Command Museum. To this day, part of the recruit training curriculum includes a trip to the museum to learn Marine Corps history. (MCRD.)

GOODHUE'S PLAN. This was architect Bertram Goodhue's original idea of the how the base would look when completed. With limited exception, the modern recruit depot looks very much like the original plan. The original 50 buildings have expanded to over 200. In 1991, the 110 acres forming the historical district of MCRD were placed in the National Register of Historic Places. (MCRD.)

COMMANDANT MAJOR GENERAL BIDDLE. Maj. Gen. William Biddle, left, was the 11th commandant of the Marine Corps from 1910 to 1914. He came from a very affluent family background in Philadelphia and was educated in some of the most prestigious institutions there. Although his tenure as commandant is considered to be one of relative quiet, he is considered the creator of the modern Marine recruit training concept. While a colonel in command of the 1st Brigade in the Philippines in 1905, Biddle conceptualized his recruit training strategy. It was General Biddle's belief that simply sending new men to be trained at Navy yards was inadequate, and he designed a formula that required recruits to be under direct supervision of a drill instructor from start to finish. While commandant in 1911, Biddle authorized the formation of recruit depots at Norfolk, Virginia; Mare Island, California; and Puget Sound, Washington. (MCRD.)

MCRD FROM THE AIR, c. 1920. This aerial view of Marine Corps Base San Diego shows five of six barracks buildings completed. The base was already beginning to assume the very stately and impressive shape that architect Bertram Goodhue had envisioned. The road in the upper right is Barnett Avenue, which is still there today. Just past the bend at the top of the picture is the current location of Sail Ho Golf Course. (MCRD.)

SECRETARY OF THE NAVY DANIELS. Josephus Daniels, secretary of the Navy from 1913 to 1921, is pictured here with San Diego congressman William Kettner (second from left) during a visit to San Diego Navy yards. Secretary Daniels considered the proposed site for the Marine base "a very desirable piece of property for the Navy to own." (MCRD.)

THE REALIZATION OF A DREAM. With his staff surrounding him, Brig. Gen. Joseph Pendleton raises the national ensign for the first time over the grounds of Marine Corps Base San Diego. General Pendleton's dream for a base in San Diego started when he was just a colonel and took over six years from inception to completion, with much of the work done by the general himself. After years of actively campaigning, processing paperwork, and lobbying for construction funds, General Pendleton's aspiration for a permanent Marine base in San Diego was made a reality on December 1, 1921. At that time, it was not known as MCRD San Diego but was officially designated as the Marine Advanced Expeditionary Base San Diego. In addition to training Marine recruits, the San Diego base was home to various combat units and follow-on schools. (MCRD.)

1ST BATTALION, 7TH MARINE REGIMENT, 1921. The 1st Battalion of the 7th Marine Regiment (1/7) was established at San Diego on April 1, 1921. During the first two decades of its history, 1/7 was disbanded, reformed, and redesignated multiple times, including its first renaming as the 1st Separate Battalion of the 5th Brigade when the 2nd Advance Base Force under General Pendleton became the 5th Brigade. Under the command of legendary Marine Lt. Col. Lewis "Chesty" Puller, 1/7 distinguished itself in the Pacific theater during World War II. John Basilone, another legend of the Corps, served under Puller during the Japanese assault of the Matinukau, in which Basilone almost singlehandedly saved the regiment with his machine gun employment. For his heroism, he was awarded the Medal of Honor. Today, 1/7, as well as the rest of the 7th Marines, are headquartered at Marine Corps Air Ground Combat Center in Twentynine Palms, California. (MCRD.)

Two

THE EARLY YEARS

1923–1939

With the move of the recruit depot to the new San Diego base, the die was cast for expansion and increased operational tempo. Tenant regiments and battalions would soon be deployed from the base to operate in various theaters such as Santo Domingo, China, and Nicaragua. The base saw many changes during this time, from the introduction of aviation units to the West Coast and headquartering of the Fleet Marine Force to the occupation of nearby lands for rifle, artillery, and tank training.

GENERAL PENDLETON REVIEWS THE BASE. In this photograph from 1923, Brigadier General Pendleton inspects his Marines, accompanied by his senior staff, local commanders, and naval officers from various San Diego stations. Scrutiny of every detail is a hallmark of all Marine commanders, and General Pendleton was a competent and inspiring leader. (MCRD.)

RIFLE INSPECTION. In this c. 1935 photograph, a squad of Marines undergoes a rifle inspection. The Marine being inspected has opened the rifle action to "show clear" and assure the inspecting officer that he is not being handed a loaded weapon. This procedure is still in use to this day through a drill movement called "Inspection, Arms!" (MCRD.)

FIELD DAY, 1924. Some things never change, and maintaining a high state of cleanliness is no exception. In this rare informal photograph, these young men take advantage of a lull in supervision to trade military bearing for silly antics, posing with mops and brooms instead of the usual rifles and packs. (MCRD.)

CHANGE OF COMMAND, 1926. Brig. Gen. Smedley Butler (right) and Col. Alexander Williams (left) are shown at Butler's assumption of command ceremony in front of the arcade. Colonel Williams was the commander of the 4th Marine Regiment. Butler later court-martialed Williams for intoxication and conduct unbecoming a Marine officer after an incident at a party Williams hosted in honor of Butler's assumption of command. (MCRD.)

4TH MARINE SPORTS. Here, men from San Diego's own 4th Regiment pose for a basketball team photograph while deployed to China. The Marine Corps has long been involved with team sports, as it raises morale and promotes even better fitness of the participants. Nothing helps unit cohesion like a good team sport. (MCRD.)

RETURNING HOME. After eight years of expeditionary duty in Santo Domingo, "San Diego's Own" 4th Marine Regiment returns home. The Marines in this photograph have recently disembarked the transport ship USS *Henderson* and await orders to march back to MCRD. Recently retired Major General Pendleton, their former commander, was on hand to greet them. (MCRD.)

FOOTBALL AT MCRD. Sports at the San Diego Marine base were a primary reflection of the Marines' competitive spirit. Although football and baseball were the big ticket teams at MCRD, boxing, bowling, racquetball, wrestling, golf, and volleyball were also represented by official teams. Above, Don Beeson poses with football teammate Cooper in 1929. Beeson was a fixture on several base sports teams. Marine football teams, like the one shown below in the mid-1920s, were the crowd favorites, bringing thousands of civilian spectators to the games. One of the big rivalry teams for the San Diego Marines was San Diego State College. (Both, MCRD.)

TELL IT TO THE MARINES. Shown above, from left to right, are Lon Chaney Sr., Eleanor Boardman, Gen. Smedley Butler, and William Haines. *Tell It to the Marines* was a silent film made in 1926. It was filmed aboard MCRD, making it the first movie to have the full endorsement and cooperation of the Marine Corps. General Butler was asked by Metro-Goldwyn-Mayer to be the technical advisor for the film. Chaney and Butler pose, left. These two men formed a friendship during filming that lasted the rest of Chaney's life. For his extraordinary work in the film and his accurate portrayal, Lon Chaney was chosen to become an honorary Marine, the first film star given that honor. (Both, MCRD.)

PASS IN REVIEW. Above, elements of the 6th Marine Regiment pass in review in the 1930s. These weekly parades were common at San Diego and were usually followed by a reception for officers and their wives. Below, a rifle company passes in review, performing a drill movement known as "Eyes, Right." A pass in review was a way for commanders to inspect their Marines as a unit for combat fitness, efficiency, and military bearing. This tradition is continued to this day through the execution of a pass in review during specific ceremonies, such as changes of command and recruit graduations. (Both, MCRD.)

PARADE THE LINE. This parade of troops, a common scene in its day, was more than likely one of a series of command-prompted inspections of the 4th or 6th Marine Regiments. In the early days of MCRD, San Diego citizens were invited and encouraged to attend such events. The band, pictured at far left, was very active in the San Diego area. (MCRD.)

DEDICATION OF YMCA, 1924. The Marine Corps Base San Diego Band leads a formation of troops from the 4th Marines down West Broadway in downtown San Diego for the dedication of the Army and Navy YMCA. The base band was, and still is, a common sight around local events and dedications. (MCRD.)

GENERAL VANDEGRIFT. Gen. Alexander Archer Vandegrift was commissioned a second lieutenant in January 1909. Early in his career, General Vandegrift served in Nicaragua, Veracruz, and Haiti before being appointed the assistant chief of staff at MCRD under Gen. Smedley Butler in 1926. Vandegrift was personally requested by General Butler to serve in that capacity due to their friendship. General Butler was seeking "moral support" due to the lack of excitement in his position. After leaving MCRD San Diego, Vandegrift served in China and Washington, DC. He was placed in charge of the 1st Marine Division in November 1941, one month before the outbreak of World War II. General Vandegrift was commanding general of the 1st Marine Division during the attack on Guadalcanal and the Solomon Islands, where he earned the Medal of Honor for his actions there. As a lieutenant general, Vandegrift became the 18th commandant of the Marine Corps in 1944. Vandegrift was also the first Marine to become a four-star general while still on active duty in April 1945. The general left active duty in 1947. (MCRD.)

SHOOTING POSITIONS. Every Marine is a rifleman, and that will never change. What has changed, however, are the various positions from which Marines fire their rifles. In what can best be described as very high-kneeling, these men fire at an aerial target using a position that is no longer in use by the Marine Corps. (MCRD.)

ON THE LINE AT CAMP ELLIOTT. As the numbers of trainees increased, so too did the need for more space to teach them. Camp Elliott (previously referred to as Camp Holcomb) helped to satisfy the Corps' requirement for range space. Until permanent structures were built, shooters would have to stay in tents during the training cycle. (MCRD.)

MCRD, 1926. Marines in the Western Mail Guard, Detached Guard Company, prepare for duty. As many as 68 officers and 2,452 enlisted men were posted on trains, trucks, and in post offices throughout 12 of the western United States. Once the Marines were in place, only one robbery of an unguarded truck occurred. By early 1927, the men returned to base to prepare for expeditionary duty in China. (MCRD.)

WESTERN MAIL GUARDS. In 1921, a presidential order assigned Marines to provide security for the US Mail after a string of robberies and vicious attacks on postal personnel. The presence of the Marines quickly brought the violence to a halt. The robberies began again in 1926, and Marines from the 4th Regiment at MCRD were assigned to the Western Mail Guard, as was the MCRD commander, Brig. Gen. Smedley Butler. (MCRD.)

GENERAL MATTHEWS. The Marine Corps Rifle Range at La Jolla was around for many years until it was renamed after Brig. Gen. Calvin Bruce Matthews in the 1942 expansion of the Marine Corps during World War II. General Matthews was commissioned a second lieutenant in the Marine Corps in 1904. Matthews was a veteran of Panama, China, Haiti, and Nicaragua. While in Haiti, Matthews was second in command of the Haitian National Guard. When General Matthews was stationed in Nicaragua, he was placed in complete command of the local National Guard there. He was renowned for his accomplishments as an expert rifleman, serving as captain of multiple Marine national match teams and as a leading proponent of marksmanship training in general in the Marine Corps. Matthews was tragically killed in an automobile accident in August 1939, survived only by his wife, Julia. (MCRD.)

MCRD Armory, 1930s. A Marine is nothing without his or her rifle, as every Marine is a rifleman. Here, a recruit is issued his field gear by the duty armorer. All that a Marine would take into combat in the pre–World War II era was a rucksack, bandolier, bayonet, and his M1903 Springfield rifle. (MCRD.)

MCRD Barracks. This photograph was taken from behind the arcade in the early 1920s, facing southeast toward the parade grounds. Note the period vehicles and unfinished parade deck. Balboa Park is off in the distance to the left, and San Diego Bay is clearly visible on the right. (MCRD.)

MAJOR GENERAL PENDLETON. The primary military advocate for a permanent Marine base in San Diego, Maj. Gen. Joseph Henry Pendleton had a long and illustrious career in the Marine Corps. General Pendleton graduated from the US Naval Academy in July 1884 and was commissioned as a second lieutenant. As a young lieutenant, he was stationed at both of the Marine bases that performed recruit training before the creation of MCRD San Diego. Pendleton was at Marine Barracks, Mare Island, from May 1889 to May 1892. As a major, he commanded the Marine detachment at Puget Sound from September 1906 to September 1909. Before convincing the Marine Corps of San Diego's importance, he commanded Marines aboard the USS *Yankee* in the Spanish American War, where he is credited with giving the command for firing the final shot of that campaign. Upon retirement, he was appointed a major general. (MCRD.)

FLEET MARINE FORCE GENERAL STAFF, 1936. The headquarters of the Fleet Marine Force (formerly known as Advance Base Force) was moved to San Diego in the fall of 1935. This photograph, taken six months later in March 1936, shows the FMF commander, Brig. Gen. Douglas McDougal (center), also the base commander at the time. To his right is Col. Emile Moses, who, as a major, was the first recruit training commander. (MCRD.)

MCRD MAIN GATE. A lone Marine sentry stands guard at Gate 3 by the headquarters building in the late 1920s. When not fighting the enemy, Marines are often tasked with other billets, such as guard duty. The cannon in the foreground is only for show. The same guard shack remains in position to this day. (MCRD.)

UNIFORMS ON DISPLAY. The Marines in this 1925 photograph pay homage to the past by demonstrating some of the uniforms of the men who came before them. From left to right are the uniforms of the original Continental Marine, the Florida Indian War, the Civil War, the Spanish-American War, and World War I. The "current" 1925 uniforms are now considered uniforms of the past as well, but the dress and service uniforms remain very similar to modern-day issue. (MCRD.)

USS HENDERSON. This transport ship, like MCRD itself, was a frequent home of the San Diego regiments. The *Henderson* brought the 4th back from Santo Domingo in 1924, took them to Hawaii in 1925 for a joint Army-Navy exercise, and transported the 6th and 10th regiments to China to meet up with the 4th Marines. (MCRD.)

THE FLYING LEATHERNECKS. In 1924, the first aviation unit on the West Coast was organized at San Diego. Observation Squadron One (VO-1M) was transferred there from Santo Domingo, arriving August 16. VO-1M was the first Marine squadron to join an expeditionary force. Another observation and one fighter squadron were added by 1926, and by 1931, there were 18 observation and fighter planes. While the headquarters was at MCRD, the aircraft, such as the Curtiss F6C Fighters above, were stationed across the water at Naval Air Station North Island. Below is a Curtiss Falcon, also called a Douglas O2C/OC2, used by Observation Squadron 10, also stationed at San Diego. (Both, MCRD.)

M. WODARCZYK - CAPT. H.D. CAMPBELL   CAPT. R.A. PRESLEY - MAJ. ROSS E. ROWELL

FIRST FLYER. Maj. Ross E. Rowell (far right) was the commanding officer for the first Marine aviation unit on the West Coast, known as the Observation Squadron of the West Coast Expeditionary Force (VO-1M). Rowell did not enter into the aviation community until 1923, when he was already a major, but he quickly proved himself as an excellent pilot and leader. He was commended by the secretary of the Navy for his top gunnery scores and by the commandant of the Marine Corps for his success as group commander in San Diego. As commander of VO-1M deployed to Nicaragua, Rowell led his five-plane detachment of DH-4s in a dive bombing close air support mission to relieve a surrounded Marine garrison. This mission was one of the first coordinated dive bombing attacks in aviation history. For this mission, Rowell was awarded the Distinguished Flying Cross and Navy Distinguished Service Medal. (Library of Congress.)

Two Histories Being Written.
This 1927 photograph shows the *Spirit of St. Louis* just before leaving for New York and its eventual transatlantic flight that would make history. In the background is the west end of the Marine base and San Diego Bay. The marsh area that was filled can be clearly seen. More filling would eventually be needed to build the airport. (MCRD.)

Quartermaster Building. Completed in 1922, the Quartermaster storehouse building (with "Old Smokey" in the background) was the supply hub for the base. Anything related to supplies, ammunition, food, or other general logistics was handled by the base quartermaster and his office. In the modern Marine Corps, the quartermaster department is encompassed in the S-4 or G-4 staff sections, who handle all logistical matters. (MCRD.)

MARINE CORPS RIFLE RANGE LA JOLLA, 1938. In keeping with Marine Corps style, before they had a permanent home in San Diego, the Marines built a rifle range. In 1916, the Army Air Corps took over North Island, and the Marines lost their range there. The following year, the Corps leased 544 acres from San Diego and had a range built by the end of the next year. The name would later change to Camp Matthews. Below, Marines on the La Jolla rifle range take a momentary safety break from shooting to wait for the train to pass by. (Both, MCRD.)

"CORPSMAN UP!" The Marine Corps does not have its own medical personnel, so they rely on the Navy to provide doctors and medics, known as corpsmen. These men and women live, eat, and train with the Marine units to which they are assigned and therefore need to be fully versed in the ways of the Corps. Field Medical Battalion was created to train Navy medics to keep up with the rigorous demands placed on them by Marine units. In these 1930s photographs, corpsmen prepare for and execute litter drills, practicing to evacuate casualties from the battlefield. Notice the uniforms these men are wearing. Even today, Navy personnel serving with Marine units are allowed to wear Marine uniforms if they are within Marine Corps regulations. The only differences are branch-of-service identifiers and rank insignia for enlisted. (MCRD.)

GENERAL LEJEUNE. Maj. Gen. John Archer Lejeune (pronounced "le-jurn") was the 13th commandant of the Marine Corps, affectionately known as "The Marine's Marine" and the "Greatest of All Leathernecks." Upon graduation from the US Naval Academy, Lejeune completed a two-year cruise as a midshipman but chose the Marines nonetheless. In World War I, he commanded the Army's 2nd division, only the second Marine to hold an Army divisional command. General Lejeune became the 13th commandant of the Marine Corps in 1920 and served in that capacity until 1929, when he retired and assumed the office of superintendent of the prestigious Virginia Military Institute. Lejeune was commandant at the time when recruit training was moved to San Diego. He delayed the initial move from Mare Island by nine months in order to prevent "dissatisfaction" among the Marines at Mare Island. (MCRD.)

ARTILLERY PRACTICE AT CAMP HOLCOMB. The Marines pictured here are firing what was known as a 75mm Pack Howitzer, later designated as the M116. This gun was designed because of a need for a portable artillery piece that could move easily over rough terrain. It was called a pack gun because it could be broken down into pieces and packed on vehicles, animals, or a person. Camp Holcomb was the unofficial name for a large area of land leased from the City of San Diego in the Kearney Mesa area several months out of the year for artillery and machine gun practice. During World War I, the Army had occupied the same area and called it Camp Kearney. (Both, MCRD.)

GENERAL HOLCOMB. Gen. Thomas Holcomb was commissioned a second lieutenant in the Marine Corps in April 1900. As his career developed, Holcomb served in the Philippines, China, Cuba, and in both World War I and World War II. In 1936, he was appointed 17th commandant of the Marine Corps. Holcomb was the first Marine to attain the rank of full four-star general, which he received after he retired in 1944 based upon a new act of Congress that advanced officers one rank upon retirement. Holcomb actually reached mandatory retirement age in 1943, but based on his leadership and his Marine's performance in theater, President Roosevelt extended his time as commandant. During his seven-year tenure in command, the Marine Corps swelled from 16,000 to over 300,000 by war's end. (MCRD.)

Camp Holcomb. During the World War II expansion of the Marine Corps, additional buildings were constructed in the Kearny Mesa area outside of San Diego. This 1941 photograph shows what was briefly known as Camp Holcomb, named after then commandant General Holcomb. The name was quickly changed to Camp Elliott, however, as General Holcomb did not believe that a Marine base should be named after any living person. (MCRD.)

Kearny Expansion. Once the Marines had established a tent camp in the Kearny Mesa area, they set out to expand the scope of their site by bringing in additional men and material. From its humble beginning, the camp grew to consist of hundreds of tents. Note that each one is perfectly covered and aligned to the next, highlighting the discipline and uniformity of the Marines there. (MCRD.)

WESTERN PLATOON LEADERS CLASS, 1935. To meet the needs of an ever-expanding officer corps, Headquarters Marine Corps authorized the creation of two classes of officer training programs for college students, one at Quantico and one at San Diego. After two six-week summer training periods, college graduates from schools lacking Naval Reserve Officer Training Corps (NROTC)

FIELD INSPECTION. Inspections are a constant in the Marine Corps. They ensure every Marine is organized and has all of the gear that is required. In this photograph from 1937, Marines stand in line and have their field gear checked by their command. Every piece of equipment is laid out in particular order and is analyzed down to the smallest part. (MCRD.)

programs were appointed as second lieutenants in the Marine Corps Reserve. They received additional training at The Basic School (TBS) and their respective technical school. This program is still a major commissioning vehicle today, especially with reserve enlisted Marines wishing to transition to active duty. (MCRD.)

INSPECTING THE TROOPS. With his signature gait, Maj. Gen. Smedley Butler inspects his men on the parade ground in San Diego as they prepare to deploy to Nicaragua in support of the Banana Wars. This was not a standard war, but a series of military occupations in Panama, Honduras, Nicaragua, Mexico, Haiti, and the Dominican Republic in defense of American financial interests in Central America. (MCRD.)

QUARTERS ONE, 1926. Pictured are the commanding general's quarters just after completion in 1926. The first resident was Brig. Gen. Smedley Butler. Behind the home are the Butler Gardens, containing a koi pond, bamboo from Okinawa, and the Kennedy hedge, which was used as a backdrop for President Kennedy's speeches at MCRD. The residence is also used for official ceremonies, entertaining dignitaries, and weddings. (MCRD.)

OFFICER'S QUARTERS UNDER CONSTRUCTION, 1925. Although 10 were originally planned, only five quarters were ever built for married officers. These houses were constructed away from the rest of the base facilities in a sprawling park-like setting a few hundred yards behind the administration building, west of the parade ground. These five quarters now house the commanding general and other high-ranking officers from MCRD. (MCRD.)

Evening Colors at MCRD. In the early 1920s, the American flag is lowered at MCRD. Evening colors is always sounded at sundown, so the exact time it occurs varies by the season. The flagpole is still in the same place today, and colors is still performed each day at 8:00 a.m. and sunset. (MCRD.)

Initial Construction Complete. In this photograph from the early 1920s, the entire facility of MCRD can be seen as it was when it opened. In the background is the Mission Hills area to the northeast, along with what would become the corner of Barnett Avenue and Pacific Coast Highway. (MCRD.)

BOUND FOR CHINA. The 4th Marine Regiment assembles in preparation for expeditionary service in Nicaragua. While they were assembled and awaiting embarkation, their orders changed, and the regiment was directed instead to China. Under the command of Col. Charles Hill, the Marines left San Diego on February 3, 1927, never again to return as a regiment. (MCRD.)

6TH MARINES DEPART SAN DIEGO FOR CHINA. Elements of the 6th Marine Regiment board trucks that will take them to the USS *Chaumont*, bound for China. Just a few years prior, this regiment had been reactivated at San Diego, effectively replacing "San Diego's Own" 4th Regiment, which had previously deployed to China and then remained there. (MCRD.)

"OLD SMOKEY." A seemingly insignificant part of MCRD architecture, the smoke stack of the incinerator, dubbed "Old Smokey" by most San Diego residents, was something of a landmark on the San Diego base. Built in 1920 and pictured here in 1925, the incinerator was dismantled in 1955. The smokestack was finally taken down in 1975, partly because of concerns for air traffic from nearby Lindbergh Field. (MCRD.)

LOTT FIELD, 1939. The athletic field at MCRD was the first known named facility on the base. Dedicated in May 1939, Lott Field was named for Maj. Charles McL. Lott, the base athletic officer and football coach from 1935 to 1938. Under his leadership, the San Diego Marines swept the major university teams in the area, including the University of Southern California and San Diego State. (MCRD.)

BUTLER AND LEJEUNE. Brig. Gen. Smedley Darlington Butler (left) and Maj. Gen. John Archer Lejeune, two of the most notable men in Marine Corps history, pose together in their dress uniforms. Butler is one of only two Marines to be awarded two Medals of Honor. At the time of his death, Butler was the most decorated Marine in history. He received the Marine Corps Brevet Medal for heroism during the Boxer Rebellion in 1900 and his first Medal of Honor in Veracruz, Mexico, in 1914. Three years later he was awarded his second Medal of Honor for extraordinary heroism during operations in Haiti. In 1924, Butler took a leave of absence from the Marine Corps to become the director of public safety for the City of Philadelphia. His leave ended in 1926, and he returned to the Marines at San Diego. After being passed over for commandant of the Marine Corps, Butler retired in 1931. (MCRD.)

MARINE FIRES THE LEWIS MACHINE GUN. Marines at Camp Matthews train on the newly adopted Lewis machine gun. Originally rejected by the US Army, the Lewis went into production and use in Britain, and the Marines quickly found a way to implement the weapon as a light machine gun. The oversized-looking barrel is actually a hollow cooling shroud. (MCRD.)

"STANDBY . . . TARGETS!" As the saying goes, "If it ain't broke, don't fix it." In this image from 1924, Marines (or recruits) take a break from pulling and spotting targets between relays of shooters. This system is still used today at most Marine ranges. Targets are placed into "carriages" and raised and lowered manually after the round impact is spotted in the dirt behind the targets and marked on the target itself. (MCRD.)

MARINES IN SANTA BARBARA, 1925. Following the destructive earthquake in July 1925, three companies of Marines were dispatched from San Diego to Santa Barbara to maintain security and aid in rescue efforts. Within three hours of their 8:30 p.m. arrival, the Marines had set up camp at Peabody Stadium at the high school (above) and were patrolling the streets of Santa Barbara. (UC Santa Barbara.)

CAMP KEARNEY BEFORE THE CORPS. Camp Kearney was named after US Army general Stephen Watts Kearney. It was established by the Army in 1917 as a short-term processing and training center for soldiers on their way to World War I. The Marines took up the land in the 1930s and changed the name to Holcomb, then Elliot. It is now the site of Marine Corps Air Station Miramar. (MCRD.)

SHOOTING POSITIONS. At Camp Matthews in the 1940s, the shooters in this photograph are demonstrating the three low shooting positions. From left to right are the kneeling, sitting, and prone positions. The remaining position, not pictured here, is the standing, or off-hand position. These are still the standard shooting positions used on the rifle range today. (MCRD.)

WEAPON MAINTENANCE. A long-standing tradition in the Marine Corps is to fill unoccupied time with maintaining weapons. Attention to detail in keeping a clean weapon is a cornerstone principal in recruit training and is carried throughout a Marine's career. This second-nature practice served the Marines well in Vietnam and in the sandy environments of the Middle East, where the newly fielded M16 was prone to maintenance-related malfunction. (MCRD.)

PROFESSIONAL MARINE. General Pendleton dedicated 40 years of his life to the Marine Corps, starting as a 24-year-old second lieutenant. Pendleton would have stayed in the Corps longer, but he was forced out when he reached the mandatory retirement age of 64. He retired to Coronado, where he could gaze upon his crowning achievement: MCRD San Diego. (MCRD.)

Three

THE EXPANSION YEARS
1940–1971

World War II introduced a new era to Marine Corps Base, Naval Operating Base, San Diego. The wartime boom ended the Depression and created a need for a larger Marine Corps. The American people responded and enlisted in record numbers. This influx of new recruits made construction increase to accommodate the need. New camps were established, and the Corps grew to over 300,000 strong at its peak. After World War II, the Marine Corps experienced a reduction in force that prompted the base to be renamed Marine Corps Recruit Depot, San Diego. Combat troops were no longer stationed there, and MCRD would become strictly a training base from then on.

CAMOUFLAGED BUILDINGS, 1940s. During World War II, many of the buildings aboard MCRD were painted in a camouflage pattern to help protect against aerial bombardment. Because the base is located directly on the coast of California, the threat of attack from Japan was considered possible at any time. Above is the administration building, finished in 1943, which still houses the major base command offices and staff sections. Below is the base theater, also completed in 1943, which was built with a radio station that broadcasted a weekly radio program called *Halls of Montezuma*. The buildings were restored to their original state after the war. (Both, MCRD.)

SEA SCHOOL LADDERWELL. Sea School candidates were selected at the end of recruit training by their drill instructors. This was considered a prestigious assignment as a sign of their proficiency as a Marine. These recruits generally were among the top third of their graduating class to ensure the Marine Detachments were staffed with the most qualified Marines available. (MCRD.)

SEA SCHOOL, 1953. Here, Sea School graduates stand at the sea school sign located at MCRD. An assignment to a shipboard Marine Detachment was considered a privilege, and only a small number of Marines were selected to such duty. Sea School, the oldest school in the Marine Corps at the time, had been a landmark at MCRD for over 60 years before graduating their last platoon on December 8, 1987. (MCRD.)

PRESIDENT KENNEDY VISITS MCRD, JUNE 1963. Above, Pres. John F. Kennedy inspects the Sea School honor guard during his visit to MCRD. He is accompanied by base commander Maj. Gen. Sidney Wade and Sea School commander Capt. Russell Lloyd. Below, President Kennedy greets one of the many drill instructors assembled to honor the president's visit. As a byproduct of this visit, part of the commanding general's quarters underwent a remodel. It was also during this visit to San Diego that President Kennedy was awarded an honorary doctor of laws degree from San Diego State, the first honorary degree given by a California state school. (Both, MCRD.)

MONTFORD POINT MARINES. In 1943, the first all-black Marine unit, trained at Montford Point, North Carolina, arrived at MCRD San Diego. Although their stay was short-lived, they left a positive impression on the base, due in part to their demonstration of advanced close order drill techniques, which impressed their fellow Marines. (MCRD.)

CODE TALKERS. In May 1942, the first all-Indian Marine platoon arrived at San Diego. These Navajo men were recruited to use their native language as an unbreakable code on the battlefield. While at San Diego, they were reported to be disciplined and skilled at a level far superior to the average recruit. (MCRD.)

ANTI-AIRCRAFT GUNNERY INSTRUCTION, 1940s. Students at Sea School receive instruction on employing anti-aircraft machine guns. Above are M1917A1 water-cooled Browning machine guns, which were used against air targets. Variants of this machine gun were used up through the Vietnam War. As demonstrated by the attacks on Pearl Harbor, large ships were easy targets for enemy aircraft, and the best defense aside from friendly fighters was a Marine behind an anti-aircraft machine gun. Below in 1944 are students practicing loading and unloading drills with another anti-aircraft weapon, the Oerlikon 20mm. Many of these kinds of weapons, as well as various other historical guns, are still on display at MCRD San Diego today. (Both, MCRD.)

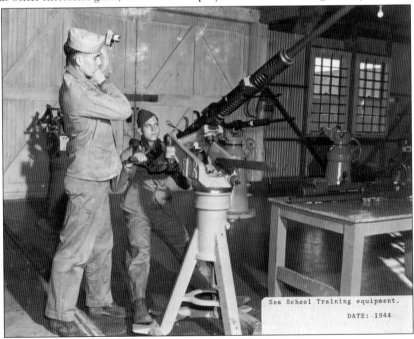

RANK STRUCTURE. In this photograph, Sea School students learn the equivalent rank structure used in the Navy and their various insignias of rate and grade. Depending on a sailor's specific job, he or she may wear insignia that is somewhat different than other sailors of the same grade. This is important to distinguish when addressing a sailor by his or her rank/rate. (MCRD.)

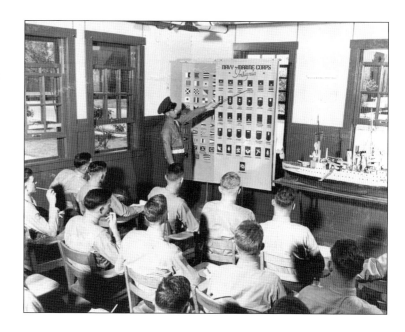

SHIP FAMILIARIZATION. Sea School students receive a class on recognizing the various compartments and areas of a ship. In this photograph, a clear mock-up of an Essex or Independence class aircraft carrier is disassembled deck-by-deck to demonstrate the complexity of the interior of a ship. Navigating the maze of passageways and decks on ship can be overwhelming if not prepared. (MCRD.)

FIVE-INCH DECK GUN. Marines practice gunnery drills on the "5/51" five-inch deck gun at MCRD in 1936. One of the essential tasks of the Marine Detachment aboard naval vessels was crewing the guns. These drills were performed over and over until every Marine knew every job and each component without fail. These guns were used against ground targets as well as enemy ships. (MCRD.)

ANTI-AIRCRAFT GUN. Vital to ship security, Marines at MCRD learn how to use the water-cooled .50 caliber machine gun. World War II changed naval warfare, as airpower was used extensively in sea battles. Many times the opposing armadas never met, relying completely on air superiority. This made anti-aircraft gunnery one of the more vital roles Marines played on ship. (MCRD.)

RED MIKE. Maj. Gen. Merritt "Red Mike" Edson was most well known for his command of the 1st Raider Battalion (also known as Edson's Raiders) in World War II, where he earned the Medal of Honor and his second Navy Cross. Edson was a leading advocate of small arms marksmanship training and was heavily involved with competitive Marine teams. He was a firing member of the winning rifle team in 1921, coach for rifle and pistol in 1927, 1930, and 1931, and the team captain and coach for the Marine rifle teams in 1932 and 1933. After retirement, Edson was the first commissioner of the Vermont state police, his home state, and executive director of the National Rifle Association. The recruit rifle range and field training facility at Camp Pendleton, officially considered a part of MCRD, is named in his honor. (MCRD.)

ARTILERY MARINES IN SAN DIEGO, 1940. These young men from the 10th Marine Regiment stand for a photograph with their artillery piece near the athletic fields on MCRD. The 10th Marines were split out of Quantico, Virginia, and the second battalion was sent to San Diego to serve with the 6th Marine Regiment. (MCRD.)

LONG HIKE TO CAMP PENDLETON. Men from the newly reformed 9th Marine Regiment make the nearly 40-mile march to their new home on Camp Pendleton from their former base on Camp Elliott. These San Diego–based Marines would be the first unit to occupy the new premier training base in the Marine Corps, named after longtime San Diego base advocate Maj. Gen. Joseph Pendleton. (MCRD.)

DRILL INSTRUCTOR (DI) SCHOOL. During World War II, a school was created to prepare new drill instructors for the rigors of DI duty. Initially only a few weeks long, it was expanded to 10 weeks in 1947. During the Korean War, it was shortened to 3 weeks due to the shortage of instructors, but since then it has been 11 weeks. This photograph shows a graduating class from 1953, before the infamous campaign cover was introduced. (MCRD.)

INSTRUCTORS SCHOOL CLASS 21
7 AUGUST 1953

THE CAMPAIGN COVER. Once a standard uniform item, the campaign cover, affectionately known as the "Smokey Bear," was worn by every Marine up through the 1940s. As time passed, the cover was recalled in favor of more tactical headgear. In 1956, the campaign cover was reintroduced as a uniform item, this time exclusively for drill instructors. In this 1971 photograph, Marines at Drill Instructor School listen to an experienced DI. (MCRD.)

WORLD WAR II EXPANSION. The Marine Corps' numbers expanded to over 300,000 at the peak of World War II. To augment the additional training area needed, Camp Elliott was established in the Kearny Mesa area. Originally billeted in the soft tents pictured on the left, recruits and other Marine trainees would eventually move into the large H-style barracks being constructed. (MCRD.)

CAMP MATTHEWS. Originally Marine Rifle Range La Jolla, Camp Matthews was a sprawling range complex located on what are now the grounds of University of California, San Diego. Camp Matthews was named after Brig. Gen. Calvin Matthews, a notable marksmanship proponent in the Marine Corps. With Edson Range opening in 1964, Matthews closed, and the land was given to the state. (MCRD.)

TENT CITY, 1941. World War II increased the pace of recruit training and flooded the depot with hundreds of new recruits every day. The recruit depot originally occupied only Buildings 1, 2, and 3 along the arcade but tents started going up in 1937. By 1941, over 1,100 sixteen-man tents were erected, and by the end of 1944, the southern portion of the parade ground was a solid block of tents from east to west. The tent city was taken down at the end of World War II but was brought back again during the Korean War, although on a slightly smaller scale. (Both, MCRD.)

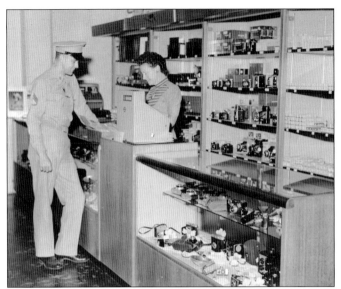

POST EXCHANGE CAMERA SHOP. A staff sergeant chats with the clerk in the camera department of the MCRD exchange. The military exchange is equivalent to a civilian department store, encompassing everything a service member would need, from clothing and cosmetics to electronics and sporting goods. One of the benefits of shopping on base is the local tax exemption. (MCRD.)

DRIVE-THROUGH SERVICE, 1966. Even the Post Exchange (PX) was getting into the drive-through craze of the 1960s. The concept of the "7-day store" (a PX open everyday) was so popular that a drive-up window was added for convenience. This express service was for shoppers getting the necessities such as milk, bread, and of course—beer, which occupied half of the menu. (MCRD.)

FEEDING THE TROOPS. Efficiency was the name of the game during wartime. This 1946 photograph shows the "Slice Master" automated bread packaging machine in the MCRD bakery. At the peak of performance in 1942, the bakery at San Diego was baking and packaging over 12,000 loaves of bread each day. (MCRD.)

MCRD NEWSPAPER OFFICE. Most every installation in the Marine Corps has a publication of some kind, and MCRD San Diego is no exception. The *Chevron* newspaper is the printed extension of the public affairs office at MCRD. The gentleman on the right is smoking his pipe indoors, a practice that has been banned by the Department of Defense since 1994. (MCRD.)

GETTING THRASHED IN THE PIT. Incentive training, commonly known as "thrashing," is a common disciplinary tool used by drill instructors to "reward" recruits for poor performance. More often than not, getting thrashed is a reward for any performance, good or bad. Although it may not seem like it to the recruits, drill instructors follow strict guidelines when implementing incentive training. (MCRD.)

PHYSICAL TRAINING, 1940. Physical training (PT) has always been paramount in the Marine Corps. Physical fitness makes for better warriors, and nothing makes for better warrior training than rifle PT. By combining physical fitness with rifle familiarization, the Marine recruit learns how to use his rifle as a weapon of opportunity while maintaining his body in perfect shape. (MCRD.)

RIFLE MANUAL. Here a platoon of recruits march with their Springfield M1903 rifles on the parade deck at MCRD in early 1940. They are being led by a drill instructor carrying the M1859 Marine NCO Sword. Notice that every man is wearing a campaign cover, as was standard issue up through World War II. (MCRD.)

DRILL. Taken during the World War II expansion, this photograph depicts recruits performing the drill movement "Dress right, dress," where each recruit in the squad extends his left arm out to the adjacent recruit's shoulder. Except for the squad leaders, everyone looks to the right so they can align themselves. Once positioned, "Ready/Front/Cover" is called, and they align to the front, putting every recruit the same distance apart. (MCRD.)

CARGO NET OBSTACLE, 1954. Recruits will encounter all sorts of obstacles while navigating the confidence course. The cargo net climb harks back to a time when netting such as this was used to reach the heights of a ship's rigging. When the Continental Marines were first formed, they were assigned as riflemen aboard ships and distinguished themselves as expert marksmen. (MCRD.)

THE "O" COURSE. The obstacle course has long been an anchor for Marine Corps training. There is no better tool to cultivate the courage of young men than conquering seemingly impossible obstacles. Taken in the 1940s, this photograph highlights the simplicity of the earlier course, with the use of climbing ropes and wooden walls. (MCRD.)

"**Shazam!**" Many parts of the popular 1960s sitcom *Gomer Pyle, USMC* were filmed on location at MCRD during its run from 1964 to 1969. Here, the stars, Jim Nabors (left), who played Gomer, and Frank Sutton (right), who played Gomer's drill instructor and platoon sergeant, pose with a Marine DI. Because the Marine Corps thought the show would do well for its image, the production company was given complete access to the base. (MCRD.)

The Marines Fly High. The Marine Corps agreed to allow filming on MCRD when approached for the 1940 film starring Lucille Ball and Richard Dix. In this photograph, supporting actress Steffi Duna (leaning on the rail) takes direction during the football game scene. Actual Marines and sailors were used as extras. (MCRD.)

PROPERTY MANAGEMENT, 1944. A gunnery sergeant and a Women's Reserve private inventory and inspect furniture and other miscellaneous property in a warehouse cage. The property management Marines controlled the inventory of garrison items such as band equipment, furniture, machinery, and even the props used in the filming of movies aboard the base. (MCRD.)

MCRD THEATER PRODUCTIONS. With a world war looming, Marine brass searched for a way to boost morale and in 1943 opened the base theater. Hosting weekly radio shows and live performances, it could seat over 2,500 spectators. This 1944 photograph depicts a comic scene between a military policeman and another actor. (MCRD.)

SAN DIEGO CHAMPIONSHIP TEAMS. Football was not the only sport on the base to bring home the glory. Swimming, baseball, volleyball, and softball teams have all recorded championship victories for the base. The San Diego volleyball team, above, took home the 11th Naval District Championship in 1930. Kneeling on the far right is Don Beeson. In addition to football and volleyball, Beeson was the 1929 tennis champ for the district and also led the baseball team in the inter-county league in 1930 with a .438 batting average. Beeson field was named in his honor in 1950. Below is the Women's Reserve softball team in 1945, the year that they also became 11th Naval District champions. (Both, MCRD.)

WOMEN'S RESERVE. A Women's Reserve (WR) Battalion was formed at San Diego in December 1943. The WRs were assigned primarily as secretaries, office clerks, and in various motor transport billets, such as drivers and gas station attendants. Female Marines were given their own area on the base, located on an old athletic field, separate from the men. They had their own medical facility, as well as messing and exchange activities and their own basketball court and softball fields. They even had their own area at the range at Camp Matthews, although they never fired weapons for qualification there. By May 1946, the last WR was discharged and the battalion was officially disbanded. (Both, MCRD.)

RECEIVING BARRACKS, 1944. Like many other buildings around MCRD, the receiving barracks was also camouflaged during the war. This building was used to house recruits when they first arrived prior to assignment to a training company. The new receiving building encompasses classrooms, offices, squad bays, and the main processing center. (MCRD.)

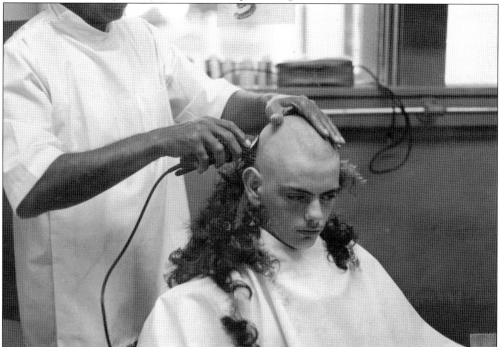

OFF WITH THEIR HAIR! Within the first 24 hours of their arrival at the depot, recruits have their heads shaved to the scalp. This serves a dual purpose. Not only does it prevent the transmission of lice, it is one of the first steps in stripping away the personal identity of a new recruit and putting him on the same level as his fellow platoon members. (MCRD)

CLOSE ORDER DRILL. Left, recruits undergoing a platoon drill inspection in the 1960s perform a drill movement called "Present Arms" while being evaluated by a drillmaster. The platoon below is marching in column at port arms. In the background is Building 31, the administration and headquarters building. Close order drill is a major component of recruit training, occupying nearly one-fifth of the training schedule. Recruit platoons are formally evaluated twice during boot camp. Drill is instrumental in teaching discipline by instilling habits of precision and instant willingness and obedience to orders, which is why it is given such attention during recruit training. (MCRD.)

SEA SCHOOL. As soldiers of the sea, Marines were required to possess knowledge of shipboard operations and duties specific to service aboard naval vessels. Established in 1923, Sea School was designed to prepare Marines for duty afloat. Their responsibilities included ship security, manning the deck guns, and damage control. Above, a Marine renders a salute to an officer on the simulated ship's quarterdeck that is the entrance to Sea School. At right, recent graduates pose by the sign leading to Sea School in 1953. This was the oldest school in the Marine Corps, operating for over 64 years with only a short break in service at the beginning of World War II. (Both, MCRD.)

FRINGE BENEFITS. Not everything in the Marine Corps has to be hard work. These two lucky Sea School students were chosen as the escorts for this "Fairest of the Fair" beauty pageant contest at the Del Mar Fairgrounds in the late 1950s. From 1942 to 1943, the Del Mar Fairgrounds and racetrack were home to Camp C.J. Miller, where MCRD and Camp Pendleton Marines underwent advanced physical training and paratrooper practice. (MCRD.)

KNOT-TYING INSTRUCTION. An important skill that every good sea soldier should possess is the ability to tie sturdy knots. When seas become rough, any unsecured gear or equipment can quickly become a dangerous projectile. This staff sergeant helps his Sea School students during their knot-tying practice time in 1940. (MCRD.)

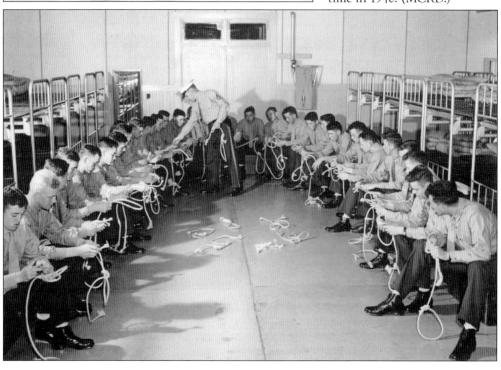

RECRUIT LAUNDRY DAY. Until around 2004, Marine recruits washed almost all of their laundry by hand and line dried it, weather permitting. The wash racks pictured here in the 1950s are the same essential design as the ones the authors washed their laundry on when they were in boot camp. Recruits were issued scrub brushes, liquid detergent, and clothespins when they arrived in San Diego. (MCRD.)

ATTENTION TO DETAIL. From the first day of training, recruits are taught to be perfectionists. Their uniforms must pass rigorous inspections where everything, even their shoes, are checked for discrepancies. In the 1960s, these recruits polish their leather dress shoes until they sparkle. The same care was taken with combat boots until 2003, when rough leather boots became standard issue. (MCRD.)

SERIES COMMANDER INSPECTION. Inspections are constant in the Marine Corps, but there are three that are required in order to successfully complete recruit training. The first is the senior drill instructor inspection, done within the first month of training. The inspection during the second month is the series commander inspection, which the recruit from the seventies in this photograph is preparing for. The final test is the battalion commander inspection. (MCRD.)

PFC DRILL INSTRUCTOR. As the need for drill instructors increased during the Korean War, Marines who had only just graduated were sometimes assigned to DI duty. In this photograph from 1953, the DI on the right is a young private first class. The use of lower enlisted men as drill instructors ended in 1954, when new regulations made it a requirement that only noncommissioned officers could become DIs. (Bob Holmes.)

"Up North." Edson Range officially opened on August 22, 1964, with the closing of Camp Matthews. Named for Gen. Meritt "Red Mike" Edson, the range facility is actually located north of MCRD on Camp Pendleton, although it is still officially an annex of the recruit depot. Recruits conduct all weapons and field training aboard Edson Range, including the Crucible. (MCRD.)

Camp Elliott. General Holcomb renamed the Kearny Mesa facility Camp Elliott after the 10th commandant of the Marine Corps, Maj. Gen. George Elliott. It augmented training there, assuming control of training replacements for combat overseas during World War II. This photograph shows the main gate to Camp Elliott during the height of the war. (MCRD.)

WOMEN RESERVES BUY WAR BONDS. Even though Marines were directly contributing to the war effort by their own service, many took advantage of offers to buy war bonds during World War II. Over the course of the war, 85 million Americans purchased over $185 billion in war bonds. Bond values ranged from $25 to $1,000. (MCRD.)

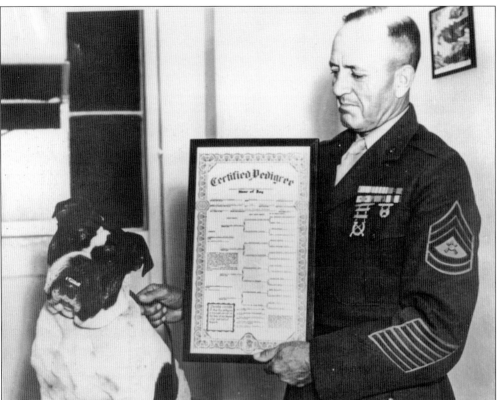

DUFFY'S LIMEY GROG. The Marine Corps has long used English bulldogs as its official mascot, ever since Gen. Smedley Butler used one for the Quantico Marine sports team in 1921. He chose the English bulldog due to its strong build and aggressive attitude. The first MCRD mascot was named James Jolly Plum Duff, who served from 1939 to 1944. His son, Duffy's Limey Grog, was the second mascot, pictured here. (MCRD.)

BAYONET TRAINING, 1944. Recruits learn the art of close combat with a bayonet and rifle. The instructor demonstrates how to parry an opponent's attack and counter with a straight thrust, which is the most deadly move that can be made. The typical areas to strike are the face and neck, chest, or the groin. (MCRD.)

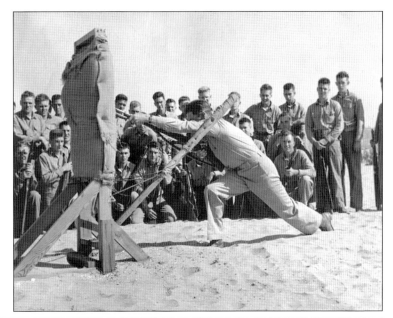

HAND-TO-HAND COMBAT TRAINING, 1955. When everything has gone wrong and his rifle is empty or missing, a Marine is still expected to stay in the fight. That is why martial arts training is a vital part of recruit training. Here, an instructor demonstrates a hip-throw movement on an unsuspecting recruit. (MCRD.)

LEARNING THE ROPES, 1958. Physical fitness is a cornerstone of Marine Corps life and training. These recruits are trained to utilize strength as well as technique to overcome obstacles that may be encountered in a combat environment. Although the knots have disappeared, the ropes remain a fixture at the end of the basic Marine Corps obstacle course. (MCRD.)

ONE MIND, ANY WEAPON. Marines are trained to be ready to fight at any time with any weapon at their disposal. Marines are riflemen first, but they must be able to make do with what they have. With Mission Hills as a backdrop, this photograph depicts a close combat instructor executing a rear leg kick, showing the proper area to strike for maximum effectiveness. (MCRD.)

MCRD GRADUATION. After the conclusion of the Korean War, the Marine Corps reduced its numbers significantly. Graduating recruit companies were much smaller, such as this one at the MCRD theater in the late 1950s. The friends and family in this photograph are seeing their young Marines for the first time in almost three months. With such dramatic transformation during training, many parents initially experience trouble identifying their own son. (MCRD.)

RECRUITS PURCHASE BOOT CAMP PHOTOGRAPHS, 1947. A time-honored tradition in the Marine Corps is commemorating important events and occasions through pictures. Boot camp is the defining moment in a Marine's life, and that first image of himself in the dress blue uniform is one that no recruit wants to leave without. (MCRD.)

Typewriter Mechanic's Course. The Marine Corps has its own way of doing everything, including repairing typewriters. This course also included teletype and adding machines, like the one pictured on the right. Like many other occupational fields and specialties, typewriter mechanics were eventually phased out and the work subcontracted to civilians. (MCRD.)

Signal Battalion. This communications student operates a hand-cranked generator that powers various kinds of radio equipment. Students at this school were taught everything from telephone repair to radio systems to semaphore. Signal Battalion was the precursor to the formal Communications and Electronics School that is now located in Twentynine Palms. (MCRD.)

READY FOR ANYTHING. These recent Sea School graduates and their squad leader stand at attention with their sea bags and rifles ready to deploy wherever the Corps will direct them. This particular squad is going to be attached to the USS *El Dorado*, a Mount McKinley class amphibious force command ship. (MCRD.)

SERVICE UNIFORM ISSUE. These recruits in the 1960s are receiving the issue of service and dress uniforms. The funny-looking thing on their heads is the frame for the white barracks and green service covers worn with different uniforms. A different color cover, or crown, can be stretched over the wire frame depending on the appropriate uniform to be worn. (MCRD.)

DEDICATION OF HALL FIELD. The football field at MCRD was named after Brig. Gen. Elmer Hall on November 17, 1956. Hall was a football legend in the Marine Corps, especially MCRD. General Hall played ball as a Marine from 1917 to 1925 and coached 1919 to 1940. He was instrumental in defining the San Diego football program and coached the first undefeated season in 1939. (MCRD.)

SHELTER HALF INSPECTION. With Mission Hills in the distance, recruits stand in formation around a shelter half during the 1940s. The shelter half is designed so the duty of carrying the entire tent is split between two Marines. One half can still be used as a lean-to if necessary. Shelter halves are still used in recruit training today. (MCRD.)

RECRUITS RECEIVE THEIR SEA BAG ISSUE. The first few days of recruit training are called the receiving phase. It is during this time that recruits are given their final medical, dental, and administrative screenings. Once declared fit for training, recruits pass through a series of supply warehouses, where they receive their uniforms, equipment, and weapon. (MCRD.)

RECRUITS RECEIVE JOB ASSIGNMENTS. In this 1947 photograph, recruits receive their Military Occupational Specialty (MOS) classification based on aptitude testing and the desires of the individual. While every effort was made to accommodate requests, the needs of the Marine Corps ultimately determined job placement. Today, most recruits leave for boot camp with their occupational fields already written into their contracts. (MCRD.)

AERIAL VIEW OF MCRD, 1942. Marine Corps Base, San Diego is pictured from the west. The H-shaped barracks buildings to the left are where the Women's Reserve Battalion was billeted. Up and to the right of those buildings was the start of the tent city that would eventually occupy that entire side of the parade ground. (MCRD.)

Four

CONTINUING LEGACY
1972–PRESENT

The conclusion of the Vietnam War brought a new challenge to the Marine Corps, as the military transitioned into an all-volunteer force. MCRD San Diego still functioned as a recruit training base, but with reduced numbers. The 1980s brought additional construction, and many of the older facilities were torn down to make room for larger and more efficient buildings. This was done to modernize the base and streamline training. Just as a Marine constantly adapts to a given mission, so does MCRD San Diego. Today, basic training is the most rigorous and comprehensive of all the US military services.

WHERE IT ALL BEGINS. The first order a new recruit receives when arriving in San Diego is to get off the bus. The second order is to get into formation on these footprints, where recruits receive their very first class on the position of attention and an introduction to the military justice system. (MCRD.)

INTIMIDATION FACTOR. In this modern photograph, the recruits of Bravo Company sit at attention with their senior drill instructors. To maintain order and discipline, even when a recruit sits down, he or she is made to sit up straight, left leg over right leg, left hand on left knee, and right hand on right knee. (MCRD.)

THEY DON'T NEED A THING. One of the first steps in the recruit training process at MCRD is contraband verification. Fresh recruits are taken straight off the bus into a room swarming with drill instructors. The recruits are made to empty their pockets and place everything on the red table in front of them. Anything deemed unfit is promptly thrown away. (MCRD.)

IF IT WERE EASY, EVERYONE WOULD DO IT. Drill instructors use booming voices and threatening gestures to create stress training. This is done to simulate the stress of combat, because if a recruit cannot handle the tension in boot camp, they would never survive in combat. This photograph shows training day one, also known as Black Friday, where new recruits are harshly indoctrinated to the recruit lifestyle. (MCRD.)

"GAS! GAS! GAS!" Above, recruits in 1955 learn the basic features and functions of their M3/M4 lightweight service gas masks. Recruits must learn to "don and clear" their masks quickly and without hesitation. They are tested on this skill in the "confidence chamber," which is a cinder block building filled with CS (chemical smoke) gas designed to show recruits and Marines that their gear is effective. Below are modern-day Marine recruits with their M40 field protective masks as they exit the gas chamber. Despite practice and classes, it is inevitable that a few recruits will still experience the effects of the gas, such as coughing, tearing of the eyes, and burning throats. (Both, MCRD.)

GENERAL DAY. A "Mustang" officer (one who serves as an enlisted man before commissioning), Maj. Gen. James Lewis Day originally joined in the Marine Corps in 1943. As an enlisted man, Day earned the Medal of Honor as a corporal for his heroic actions in Okinawa during the Battle for Sugar Loaf Hill in World War II. After completing his bachelor's degree in political science, Day completed the Basic School and commissioned as a Marine second lieutenant in 1952. General Day served in the Korean War with 1st Battalion, 7th Marines and 1st Reconnaissance Company before becoming operations officer and assistant commander at MCRD San Diego in 1956. After departing MCRD, Day was stationed at Quantico as an instructor. He deployed to Vietnam in 1966 as commanding officer of 1st Battalion, 9th Marines. Maj. Gen. James Lewis Day is one of a small group of men who saw combat in World War II, Korea, and Vietnam. (MCRD.)

MCRD Command Museum. The Command Museum aboard MCRD was opened in 1987. Since that time, nearly three million visitors, including recruits and their families, have stepped back in time and learned about the storied history of the Marine Corps. With over 25,000 photographs in the archives, the MCRD Command Museum was instrumental in the formation of this book. (MCRD.)

Recruit Training Facility, Burke Hall. Building 626 was dedicated on June 30, 1988. It was named in honor of Vietnam Medal of Honor recipient Pfc. Robert C. Burke. This training building houses several independent auditoriums that can be opened as one or sectioned off. On Sunday, the auditoriums convert to places of worship. Recruits often will attend church just to get away from their drill instructors. (MCRD.)

THE PAST COMES ALIVE. Built into the training schedule at MCRD is a trip to the Command Museum at the James L. Day Hall. Held during the first month of training, recruits are able to let loose for the first time and listen to Marine veterans as they learn about exploits of the past. Clearly in first phase, the recruits in this photograph have not yet earned the right to wear combat boots. (MCRD.)

PROFICIENCY TEST. By completion of recruit training, there are many skills that the recruit must know before he or she can earn the title US Marine. In this photograph, a young recruit demonstrates his mastery of the M16A2 service rifle. A Marine must be able to assemble and disassemble his rifle in moments, and the rifle must be immaculately clean. (MCRD.)

MCRD LIVING QUARTERS. The open squad bay, left, was typical living for single Marines at Marine Corps Base San Diego. Each man had a bed (called a rack), a wall locker, and a place to secure his rifle. This photograph highlights how little privacy the individual Marine had in the barracks. Open squad bays were the norm until the mid-1980s. Recruits in boot camp still live in a similar open configuration as seen below. Once out of initial training, single Marines in the fleet are typically assigned a one-, two-, or three-man room similar in style to a college dorm room. (Left, MCRD; below, Mackel Vaughn Photography.)

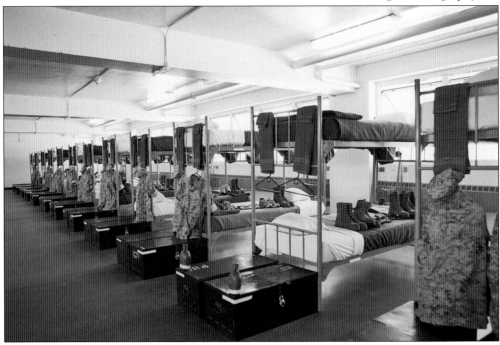

RECRUITER'S SCHOOL. In this staged photograph from 1976, a recruiting school student performs practical application with another Marine posing as a potential recruit. A recruiter must be able to articulate the benefits of military service while avoiding military jargon, a practice that is vital to the success of the student. (MCRD.)

QUONSET HUT TEARDOWN, 1990. After many decades of service to the depot, these Quonset huts are finally being razed to make way for more construction. During World War II, Korea, and Vietnam, hundreds of these buildings were constructed to handle to immense loads of recruits passing through on their way to the various theaters. (MCRD.)

ENDLESS TRANSFORMATION. Even though the initial structures on the base were completed back in 1921, MCRD will never be complete. Construction is an ongoing process, as the demands required for living and training fluctuate. As the years progressed, more facilities were required, while other facilities simultaneously became obsolete. Above, scaffolding is still in place as new barracks are being built in the 1930s. Below, additional bachelor enlisted quarters are being built in the early 1980s. From 1980 to 1989, there were 17 new structures installed, including a new police station, fire station, receiving barracks, and Burke Hall, where all recruits take their classes. To this day, construction continues with more new facilities on MCRD. (Both, MCRD.)

THE SAME, YET VERY DIFFERENT. As one moves between the buildings of MCRD, each one appears to be of the same construction and time period. Styled after Bertram Goodhue's original Spanish Colonial Revival design, every new structure on the base has a uniform appearance. This helps make the new buildings seamlessly blend with the old. Above, the officer's club is being built in the 1930s primarily using wood as a base before the stucco is applied. Below, new buildings are being constructed in the 1980s using cinder blocks. The two eras had vastly different construction techniques, but the finished products were remarkably similar. (Both, MCRD.)

MCRD IN TRANSITION. This photograph shows the eastern side of the parade deck in the mid-1970s. The Quonset huts on the right were soon to be torn down and replaced by three-story squad bays. The two tennis courts were used by permanent personnel only. (MCRD.)

MCRD AERIAL, 1985. By this time, much of the World War II– and Vietnam-era tents and Quonset huts have been removed. The tents have turned into the obstacle course area and the huts have given way to three-story squad bays. The parade deck itself has transformed a bit as well; it has been constrained to allow more room for drill instructors and permanent personnel to park their vehicles. (MCRD.)

TOWER OF TERROR. For recruits with a fear of heights, the 50-foot rappel tower is certainly one of the toughest training evolutions they will face in boot camp. Recruits are taught to fashion their own harness, called a "Swiss Seat," from a three-meter climbing rope, which they must use when they descend the tower. The old wooden structure to the right, shown here in the 1980s, was replaced in 1992 by the modern concrete tower seen below. Included in the new design was an improved stairway in lieu of the old ladder, a larger platform, and an additional capability to perform "fast-rope" training. (Right, MCRD; below, Mackel Vaughn Photography.)

WEAPONS OF OPPORTUNITY. These recruits in the 1970s are learning to utilize whatever means necessary to overcome an opponent. The young men above are learning how to execute rear cross-hand chokes using a piece of rubber hose. Several Confidence Course obstacles can be seen in the background. Pictured below is a heated sparring session between a recruit using a pugil stick to simulate a rifle with fixed bayonet and a recruit wielding a club or baton in the form of a rubber hose. Even in modern warfare with long-range weapons, a Marine must be prepared to fight with his hands or improvised weapons when all other means have failed him. (Both, MCRD.)

SOLDIERS OF THE SEA. Marines, inherently naval in character, are expected to operate in the world's littoral regions and other aquatic environments. Swim qualification is an integral component of recruit training, designed to equip Marines with the requisite skills to negotiate water obstacles and survive emergency situations involving water. Marine combat water survival training currently requires recruits and Marines to be able to swim with full gear, uniform, and weapons, as demonstrated by the recruit below. Ever conscious of safety, a drill instructor is always present (below), and a Navy corpsman can be seen above, leaning on the fence in all white. (Both, MCRD.)

BRIDGE OVER TROUBLED WATER.
Pugil stick training is designed to simulate hand-to-hand combat using a rifle with an affixed bayonet. Recruits are given instruction on proper offensive and defensive rifle bayonet tactics and then squared off with fellow recruits to test their techniques. The water in this 1970s photograph was later replaced with sawdust in the early 1990s. (MCRD.)

OBSTACLES OF A DIFFERENT KIND.
Parris Island has inclement weather that interrupts training, and San Diego has the airport. With over 600 arrivals and departures every day, the jet aircraft noise from Lindbergh Field is responsible for constant momentary lulls in training. Many drill instructors require their recruits to yell as loudly as possible every time a jet passes overhead. (MCRD)

PHYSICAL FITNESS TEST. Every Marine must maintain his or her body in top physical condition. This begins in boot camp, where recruits learn about the physical fitness test. There are three events. This photograph depicts recruits performing the first event, crunches. For a perfect score, recruits must perform 100 crunches in two minutes, complete 20 pull-ups, and run three miles in 18 minutes. (MCRD.)

SLIDE FOR LIFE, 1980s. The confidence course evolved from simple wooden structures to truly taxing obstacles after Vietnam. At 25 feet high, the "Slide for Life" gives recruits fits as they are made to slide down a slender cable with nothing to stop their fall but cold water two-and-a-half stories below. Falling also means additional "incentive training" when they return to the squad bay. (MCRD.)

PHILLIPS HALL, MCRD FITNESS CENTER. Dedicated December 12, 1951, the MCRD gym, also referred to as Building 13, was named in honor of two Marine brothers who were both killed during the Korean War. Cpl. Richard H. and 2nd Lt. Robert Phillips were the sons of a former recruit depot chief of staff. (MCRD.)

BUILDING 1, DALY BARRACKS. Building 1 is the current home of Support Battalion and Base Combat Camera. It was one of the first buildings constructed at MCRD, but it was not dedicated as Daly Barracks until 1961. The building's namesake, Daniel Daly, was one of only two Marines to be awarded two Medals of Honor. The other Marine was Smedley Butler, who called Daly "The fightin'est Marine I ever knew." (MCRD.)

"GET UP MY ROPE!" Among one of the first training evolutions in boot camp is the rope climb. The rope is a metaphor for boot camp itself, as brute strength alone will not make for success. Following orders and using technique is what gets recruits up the rope and help them become Marines. (MCRD.)

THE CRUCIBLE. A 54-hour continuous final exam for all recruits, the Crucible is a simulated combat test in which they must navigate their way through a series of events with very little sleep or food. In this 1997 photograph, recruits must work in unison to solve Timmerman's Tank, named after a World War II Medal of Honor recipient. (MCRD.)

PROUD TO CLAIM THE TITLE. With the end of the Crucible drawing near, recruits summon the last bit of strength they have left to take on the final challenge of their arduous 54-hour test. The evolution culminates with a forced march to the top of a mountain called the Grim Reaper. Although not much to look at from afar, the ever-changing slope and grade gives even the strongest legs a workout. When they have finally reached the summit, a ceremony awaits that will forever change each of their lives. It is on the top of this hill overlooking Edson Range and the scenic Pacific Ocean where each young man receives his Eagle, Globe, and Anchor emblem, officially welcoming him to claim the title of US Marine. The Crucible and Grim Reaper hike have been a part of recruit training since 1997. (MCRD.)

McDougal Hall, MCRD Base Theater. The base theater was built in 1943 and dedicated February 27, 1956. Maj. Gen. Douglas O. McDougal was the commanding general of Marine Corps Base San Diego from May 1935 until May 1937. During that same period, General McDougal was also the commanding general for the Fleet Marine Force. (MCRD.)

Worst Enemy, Best Friend. The drill instructors at MCRD treat their recruits with such ferocity and intensity that the last thing any recruit thinks at the beginning of recruit training would be rushing to shake the hand of his tormentor upon graduation. Yet, time and again, the first man each new Marine wants to greet first is his drill instructor. (MCRD.)

RECRUITS RECEIVE THEIR FIRST CLASS. Receiving drill instructor Sergeant Smith explains some of the more crucial articles of the Uniform Code of Military Justice. Receiving drill instructors are considered to be "on quota." That is, they are on a break from the much higher-paced assignments of training recruits for the whole period of boot camp. Some other quota jobs include swimming and martial arts instructor positions. (MCRC.)

THE EAGLE, GLOBE, AND ANCHOR. Then commandant, Brig. Gen. Jacob Zeilen, appointed a board to recommend a new emblem for the Marine Corps. With their suggestion, the "EGA" was adopted and has been the emblem of the Marine Corps since 1868. The eagle symbolizes the United States, the globe stands for the Marines' global service, and the anchor pays tribute to the naval roots of the Corps. (MCRD.)

MARCH ON THE COLORS. This photograph shows the MCRD color guard marching onto the parade deck from under the main arch. The term *colors* refers to the American flag and the organizational flags or banners that represent the unit bearing the detail. Before the advent of modern communication tools, armies would carry different flags to represent the various battle elements. At the center of the organization was always the national and organizational pennant. The center flags were used as a guide to direct movements in battle. The M1 Garand rifles carried by the guards on either side are fully functional but are not loaded. Although the use of color guards is strictly ceremonial today, historically they were tasked with protecting the flag in battle, as a captured flag would often signal the defeat of those whose colors were taken. (MCRD.)

SAN DIEGO RECRUITS TODAY. At the authors' request, and with the cooperation of the MCRD public affairs office, recruit training regiment, and 1st Battalion, two drill instructors brought a squad of recruits from their training platoon to help recreate the 1923 photograph on the cover of this book. Much has changed on the base and in the Marine Corps since that first platoon stood for the camera so many years ago. Technology has made the art of war-fighting into a science with advances in weapons, uniforms, and equipment, but there is one thing that will always remain unchanged: the fighting spirit and love of God, country, and corps that is present in every recruit who accepts the challenge, and every Marine who leaves the depot 13 weeks later. It is that warrior ethos and those core values that are held so dear. Honor, Courage, and Commitment. Semper Fidelis. (Mackel Vaughn Photography.)

BIBLIOGRAPHY

Anonymous. "The Marine Corps Base at San Diego." *Leatherneck Magazine*. April 1929.

Canp, William M. "San Diego, the Paradise of the Marine Corps." *Leatherneck Magazine*. February 1933.

Champie, Elmore A. "A Brief History of the Marine Corps Base and Recruit Depot San Diego, California 1914–1962." *Marine Corps Historical Reference Publication* #9. 1962.

Davidson, Winifred. "Who Raised the American Flag in Old San Diego?" *Leatherneck Magazine*. September 1958.

Pepper, Jack. "Rendezvous With Destiny." *Leatherneck Magazine*. January 1943.

Vezina, Meredith and Marine Corps Recruit Depot Museum Historical Society. *The History of Marine Corps Recruit Depot San Diego*. National City, CA: 1997.

Wright, James N. "San Diego: Largest Marine Base." *Leatherneck Magazine*. September 1941.

DISCOVER THOUSANDS OF LOCAL HISTORY BOOKS FEATURING MILLIONS OF VINTAGE IMAGES

Arcadia Publishing, the leading local history publisher in the United States, is committed to making history accessible and meaningful through publishing books that celebrate and preserve the heritage of America's people and places.

Find more books like this at
www.arcadiapublishing.com

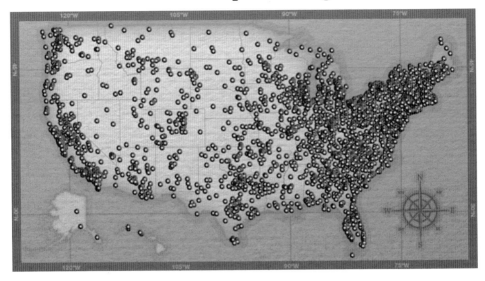

Search for your hometown history, your old stomping grounds, and even your favorite sports team.

Consistent with our mission to preserve history on a local level, this book was printed in South Carolina on American-made paper and manufactured entirely in the United States. Products carrying the accredited Forest Stewardship Council (FSC) label are printed on 100 percent FSC-certified paper.